I0559766

Finding Perfect Chaos in Your Classroom

Becoming the Teacher You Always Wanted
to Be

Dr. Ronda Blevins

Copyright © 2025 by Dr. Ronda Blevins
All rights reserved.

No portion of this book may be reproduced in any form without written permission from the publisher or author, except as permitted by copyright law.

DEDICATIONS

To my husband, David, who has supported every crazy idea I ever had – I couldn't have done this without your belief in me.

To my kids, Alyssa and Brayden, who have put up with Mom being busy and floating ideas past them – you will never know how much you have inspired me and kept me going.

To Mom and Dad who never gave up on me, even when I gave up on myself – thank you for always being there. I wouldn't have ever dreamed I would get here without you guys helping me and believing in me when I didn't believe in myself.

To the countless other family members and friends who have listened to me talk about this book for years and told me I could do it – You guys are awesome and I am so glad you are my tribe.

To the ones who gave me permission to be the teacher that I wanted to be and supported me when I had been convinced this wasn't what I was supposed to do – You can't imagine how much it has meant to have you in my corner.

And lastly, to my students – I could not be the teacher that I am without you. You guys teach me things every single day and I can't wait to see what kind of impact you are going to have in the world. Keep dreaming and creating your perfect chaos.

ACKNOWLEDGEMENTS

Writing this book has been a wild mix of excitement, doubt, late nights, and coffee-fueled writing sessions—and I couldn't have done it alone.

To my family: thank you for your patience, your love, and for cheering me on even when I wasn't sure I'd ever finish. You've been my rock through all of this.

To my friends and the people who showed up with encouragement (or distractions exactly when I needed them), I appreciate you more than you know. Thanks for listening to endless ramblings, reading drafts, and reminding me to keep going.

A special shoutout to my editing team for your guidance, feedback, and honest thoughts that helped this book become what it is.

And to you, the reader—thank you for being here. I'm so grateful you've picked up this book and given my words your time. That means the world to me.

TABLE OF CONTENTS

Change everything you are doing on the fly to meet
   the needs of your studens?
Of course I can, God called me to be a teacher

Teach without the tools you need on any given day?
Of course I can, God called me to be a teacher
Teach people that don't want to be in your class?
Of course I can, God called me to be a teacher

Take the weight of the world on your shoulders?
Of course I can, God called me to be a teacher

Exist simultaneously as the hero and the villain?
Of course I can, God called me to be a teacher

Add things to your course that don't make sense
   because it was mandated?
Of course I can, God called me to be a teacher

Love the students, even when they don't love you?
Of course I can, God called me to be a teacher

Give them a safe space to be who they are?
Of course I can, God called me to be a teacher

Take on their problems and try to guide them through
   them?
Of course I can, God called me to be a teacher

Pray for them, love them, care for them, guide them,
   lead them, and allow them to take the lead?
Of course I can, God called me to be a teacher

Take on the insurmountable task of being everything
    to everyone?
Of course I can, God called me to be a teacher

Fight against bureaucracy?
Of course I can, God called me to be a teacher

Exist in a hierarchy where I am told to be in charge,
    but also expected to let them lead?
Of course I can, God called me to be a teacher

Fight for what is best for students, regardless of the
    judgments of others?
Of course I can, God called me to be a teacher

Learn from my students while I teach them?
Of course I can, God called me to be a teacher

Can I do these things?
Can I meet the students where they are?
Can I teach them all, without judgment and bias?
Can I keep it up, day after day?
Can I give them new chances every single day,
    regardless of what they have done before?
Of course I can, God called me to be a teacher.

He called *me* to be a teacher.
The highest calling,
The one that enables the others,
The one that was so important it was modeled for us
    throughout Jesus' life.

STOP THE COMPARISONS AND IF ONLYS

The reason why we struggle with insecurity because we compare our behind-the-scenes with everyone else's highlight reel. - Steven Furtick

Have you ever looked at the classroom beside of yours, where all the students are sitting quietly and on task at their desks and been jealous? What about when you look at the people in the outside classroom or those doing the "fun" activities that seem to have so much growth happening in their rooms? Have you ever looked down your nose at another teacher's class because you thought they were in total disarray or envied the way they were able to be carefree about what was going on in the class? Have you ever compared yourself to the loud classroom, the one that is always a mess, the teacher that is always last to get their grades turned in or the supply list posted?

We live in a world that is full of comparisons and if only statements. You know them all. You've heard or said them all. "I wish my room was as put together as that one. I wish my assessments were as engaging as those. I wish my class behaved like that. I'm glad my class doesn't behave like that. I want to be a Pinterest teacher but, alas, I am an Amazon Prime teacher." Why do we do this to ourselves? We even tell our students not to play this game, yet get a group of teachers in a room and comparisons will start flying all over the place. We are taught that a great classroom is organized, well-managed, peaceful, quiet, and orderly. I think that is great, if you are the kind of teacher with the kind of students that thrives in that environment. The rest of us are just hanging out, doing the best we can, in what we have.

There has been a recurring theme in my life of chaos. Not the bad kind of chaos that is trauma filled and destructive; I was raised by normal people, have semi-normal siblings (as normal as siblings get), married a somewhat normal guy, and have 2 kids that are almost normal. No, the kind of chaos that surrounded me was the loud, boisterous, large family, sporting event kind of chaos. The kind where we got to have fun as kids, but also knew when to be serious. The kind where you could yell and play at Vacation Bible School, but in big church you had to be quiet when you colored. No, seriously, I can remember Mom and Nana both telling me I was coloring too loud on the bulletin on Sunday mornings. It wasn't my fault the paper was scratchy and I was using the little offering pencil but, I digress. I grew up in the kind of chaos that I look back on and treasure. The structured chaos that led to personal growth. Some might even say the *perfect chaos*.

Yep, there it is. *Perfect Chaos.* What do I mean by that? I think we are surrounded by beautiful and perfect chaos. I think most of us learn in chaos. And, 2 years ago, I coined the term *Perfect Chaos* when talking about education. You see, I am one of those radical thinkers that truly believes good education is steeped in relationships, engagement, activity, structure, respect, learning, and fun. I can't stand quiet and, to be honest with you, I don't even see the benefits of silence. I was that kid who was really smart, but also loved to be involved in lots of things. For me, *Perfect Chaos* is simply where all things come together to form good education.

That means it doesn't look the same in every classroom, it doesn't sound the same in every region and, as long as students are learning, it's okay if that doesn't look like tidy rows with quiet children that are focusing on their lessons. I believe perfect chaos gives us room to try and then go back and try something different if we fail. I believe it gives teachers the freedom to teach and students the freedom to learn. It implies a trust that although the process may look different, the results are going to astound you. It says that it's ok to get a little messy in the process of learning. Perfect chaos says it is okay if you didn't do as great this time, we can try a different way to learn. Perfect chaos says everyone is welcome at the table of learning. Perfect chaos says that special areas are just as useful and beneficial as core academic areas. Perfect chaos says that not everyone is supposed to go to college, we are all just supposed to be productive in using the talents we were given. Perfect chaos simply gives us the ability to admire what others are doing without falling into the comparison trap.

In this book, I'm going to share stories with you. Some are from my classrooms, some are just from life, some are from the classrooms of some of my students or my friends. I'll give you some suggestions for how to figure out what your brand of perfect chaos looks like for your classroom. I'll tell you some things that will make you laugh (hopefully) and some that might make you cry. This book is me opening my teaching style up to everyone. It is me sharing the mistakes I've made and the successes I've had. It's me laying out my educational vulnerability for the world to see. I consider myself no more of an expert than anyone else, just a teacher with a different voice to share. A voice that will hopefully give you permission and freedom to be the kind of teacher you dreamed of being, regardless of how you have to fit that into the mold developed by those in charge. You see, achieving perfect chaos can happen within the molds, strictures, and norms set forth by those in charge. Perfect chaos is simply the freedom to teach a little differently.

I've defined it (kind of) for you, but let me tell you the first story of the book. I didn't follow the traditional path to becoming a teacher. I started off in the traditional path, then made some mistakes in college (nothing felonious, just enjoyed going to football games and marching band more than all those other things I was supposed to be doing). I ended up academically dismissed. Yep, that's right. There's the first sign of chaos. I didn't know what I wanted to do or be anymore. I had realized that I couldn't fit into the Music Education mold that I was aspiring to, and I didn't know where else to turn. I think, deep down, I always knew that I would be a teacher, but what I was going to teach and how I was going to get there was all of a sudden totally unknown. So, I did what any self-respecting 19 year old would do in that situation, I got engaged to a guy that I had known for just a few months, got married right after I turned 20, and started working. Okay, technically I was working that whole second year of college, but you get the drift. I bounced (not quickly) from job to job trying to find the thing that would make me feel like me. It wasn't working in a pharmacy (although going to pharmacy school would have me sitting in a house by the lake right now instead of watching my son and my husband throw football from the carport). It wasn't being the perfect wife (my husband would definitely agree with that). I was still searching for the thing that would make me whole. So, what did we do? Well, what any married couple in that situation (you know, broke and young) would do. We had a baby. Yep, my darling daughter was born in her own version of chaos when I was just 22. It didn't take me long to figure out that I also wasn't a stay at home mom. That is no shade to stay at home moms, it just wasn't what I was supposed to do. Back to the drawing board I went and I decided that I was going to be an elementary school teacher. When she was 3, I went back to school to finish my bachelor's degree, and things were going pretty smoothly until 2 things happened. Thing number 1 was No Child Left Behind and an increase in teaching to a test instead of teaching the way students could learn. Thing number 2 was our son and the extreme chaos that he brought with him (that's a whole other book). I finally finished my BS in Sociology (don't ask how many majors I ended up trying) after taking another 2 years off to deal with my illnesses and his and went to work at our church as a graphic designer/administrative assistant. You remember that list of things that I had tried? Well, add administrative assistant to the list of things I was not very good at being. So I decided to get a Master's degree. What else do you do when you don't know what you want to do, right? I got my MS in Criminal Justice over the next year while I worked and decided I was finished. I was working at the church, my husband had left firefighting and was now in charge of Emergency Medical programs at a local community college, and I had no clue what I was going to do with my life. Then he suggested that I teach a couple of criminal justice classes at the community college to make some extra money. Within 15 minutes of my first class, I knew I had found my calling and my passion again. I was going to change the world through teaching Criminal Justice. It didn't take me long to figure out that adjuncting wasn't enough to pay the bills and there aren't that many CJ jobs out there in education. So I went back to school again to work on my Ed.D. in a brand new program, at a university in my home town, where I had sworn just 15 years earlier I would never go. In the process of finishing that, I got some really neat opportunities to teach and present and finally made the move to teach CJ in high school. I loved that, but still felt like something was missing. It was great, and I will cherish my high school students until the day that I die, but I was still missing something. Just a year after finishing my Ed.D., I was cut from my school. Now what? Was I wrong all this time? Was the work that I had done to become a teacher wrong? How could the happiness and joy I felt when I taught not mean I was where I was supposed to be?

Remember that school I swore I would never go to when I was in high school? They needed an academic advisor. I needed to find my way again. So, I took a temporary job for 90 days that turned into 3ish years of advising and then moving into the role of full-time faculty in Education. That seems like a massive understatement of what actually happened, though. You see, when I lost my previous position, I was convinced I wasn't a good teacher. When my bosses asked me to teach a class, I was convinced I needed to teach like they did. When I thought back to the teachers that I had growing up and all through school (and life), I had the picture in my head of what I was supposed to be. The problem with that was that wasn't what I am. I remembered my teachers as extroverts, commanding a classroom, loving their students, demanding respect, and incredibly knowledgeable. The problem was that I am an introvert. I hate being in places where I don't know people. I hate having to speak up around others. I hate the spotlight. But, I love to learn. So I started teaching for them. I tried to be like my colleagues, but it just never felt authentic. It felt uncomfortable. That is truly where perfect chaos was born. It was born through the process of accepting who I am and learning how to use who I am to make me a better teacher. I may not always know the answer, but I tell my students that if I don't know, we will figure it out together. I definitely don't have the quietest class. We definitely do things a little differently (think teaching Ed Tech outside in the grass with no technology every once in a while). What I have figured out through my journey is that there is always the "normal" way to do things, but that way doesn't necessarily fit everyone. Perfect chaos is finding the normal for you and your students. It requires stretching out of your comfort zone and being willing to mess up. It takes grace and compassion and forgiveness and energy and excitement and passion about what you are called to do with your life. How do you know when you've reached it? It's so simple, yet so difficult at the same time. In essence, it is when you feel like you are home.Who am I as a Teacher?

Think back to those early education classes. I bet you might remember that, at some point, some professor talked to you about philosophies of education. Are you remembering hearing something about those at some point in your education/career?

Okay, now, time for a pop quiz. Ha! I'm just joking, but we are going to think about what we learned about educational philosophies. Not necessarily to the specific educational philosophies, but to the what the philosophies mean. We are also going to do a little bit of reflection. You can answer these in this book, on a sheet of paper, or in your head (it just depends on how chaotic you want to be ☺).

1-Image by Rochak Shukla on Freepik

Do you consider yourself teacher-centered or student-centered in your teaching?

1. How often do you redo the lessons you have taught previously to add new activities or integrate new tools?
2. Do you prefer for your students to do guided exploration or for you to give them all of the information?
3. What do you believe about how your students can learn?
4. Describe the best learning experience you have had as a student.
5. Describe your best teaching experience.
6. What teaching strategies feel like a natural fit for you?
7. What do you believe is the purpose of education?

Now that you have done a little reflection on the way back time machine, let's think about your students. Would they consider you to be teacher-centered or student-centered? Why do you think they would choose that? How does that line up with what you wanted to be when you first thought about becoming a teacher?

Determining who you are as a teacher is almost as hard as determining who you are as a person. There are so many different options to choose from, and a lot of times we are influenced by the teachers that we have had. The most important things you have to determine before you can figure out what kind of teacher you are going to be require the type of reflection you have just finished. I've guided you through (at least if you did what I told you to do) the classroom reflection portion. Now you have to determine how your personality, energy level, and enthusiasm fit with the classroom reflection part. Fun fact, you actually don't have to be a super confident extrovert that has it all together and is uber positive about everything to be a good teacher. Perhaps, when you reflected on teachers you had in the past, you remembered teachers that were great teachers and also embodied all of that last sentence. If you are like me, that is a very daunting thought. You see, I am an introvert. I am shy. I remember seeing my teachers and being so confused because I thought I wanted to do that, but knew it wasn't my personality. I'm not very good at faking things, and I knew I would be totally exhausted if I tried to be one of those teachers. By the way, I am not being negative about those things. I think it is wonderful if you embody those qualities. My husband embodies those qualities. I just think it is important to acknowledge that you don't have to be that person to be a good teacher.

In other words, take a minute to think about all the different personalities that students might have. Yes, I really mean it. Think about it. Are all the students outgoing? I don't think they are. At least all my students aren't. One of the things that makes the chaos of the classroom perfect is when those different personalities and energy levels manage to come together at one time with a common goal. Doesn't it make sense that the quiet students need to see that teachers can be introverted or shy as well? Now, what personality traits did you come up with about yourself?

Whatever you just listed, you have to hold true to those. It is much more important for your students to see the true you than it is for you to fake a personality that is not naturally there. The students will see through that and you will make yourself miserable. Don't take that to mean that you can just go in on your bad days and be a total grouchy butt. You still have to be kind, but they will know if you are not being your true self and that will cause distrust.

So, who are you as a teacher? What are the top 5 qualities you currently have? Do those align with the teacher you wanted to be when you first wanted to be a teacher? It has been said that teaching consists of three things (I know, I questioned the only three thing as well). Those three things are changing attitudes, conveying information, and experimenting/practicing/trying things out. What would you add to that list? Since I don't believe in asking anyone to do something that I wouldn't do, I'll give you my answers to these last few questions in the form of my teacher statement.

I am a teacher. The top 5 qualities I bring to my classroom are compassion, encouragement, sarcasm, humor, and integrity. I spend the majority of my time between conveying information and experimenting/practicing/trying things out, but there is a little bit of changing attitudes involved as well (let's face it, I have to convince students that social media is not a news source).

I am a teacher. My goal is not to catch students doing something wrong, it is to make them want to do the right things for the right reasons. I spend my days thinking of new ways to convey that information so my students will better understand it.

I am a teacher. My classroom and office are safe spaces. My students can say what they need to say without fear of censure or judgement, then we will have a conversation about how to have those thoughts and feelings and still be kind and respectful. My desk drawers are full of food and the coffee is always readily flowing for those students that might need it. I listen when they cry and laugh at their jokes.

I am a teacher. I don't want you to just agree with me, I want you to form your own opinion based on non-biased facts. I want to help my students develop critical thinking skills so they are able to analyze the world around them and come to a decision about their own beliefs.

I am a teacher. It isn't a job or a career, it is the fiber of who I am. My teaching isn't dependent upon being in a classroom, I can find something to teach in every situation. I continuously learn and push my own limits to be the best teacher I have the capability to be for my students and the students they will have in the future.

What is your teacher statement? Are you where you want to be? Use the rest of this page to write your very own teacher statement and, if you aren't where you want to be in becoming that teacher, make your plan to get there. Not only do your students deserve the best, you deserve to be the best and most true form of yourself. Finding the perfect chaos in your classroom can't happen until you know how to get to this version of yourself. You are a teacher, you've got this.Respecting the Chaos

Every human being, of whatever origin, of whatever station, deserves respect. We must each respect others even as we respect ourselves. - Ralph Waldo Emerson

Have you ever sat down and though about respect? What about the difference between having respect for someone and respecting someone? What do I even mean by there's a difference between having respect for someone and respecting someone? A quick Google search of what is respect in a classroom gave me a great list of rules and procedures for students to follow. I don't really think that embodies respect in the classroom; at least it doesn't embody respect in my classroom. If you're reading this book, I'm guessing that status quo of respect in the classroom isn't resonating with you either. Here is another spot where I break from the status quo. Yep. Another chaotic statement is coming at you. In my classroom, respect goes both ways. Everyone is shown respect all the time, that is just a non-negotiable in my classroom. If I'm being honest, that is a non-negotiable in my life. I don't demand respect without giving it. I also don't demand that everyone like the way I operate. The only thing I ask for is that they respect my humanity. So what does that mean? It's simple, you don't have to like my decisions, but you do have to respect the fact that I made them. Students are free to disagree with me (in fact, I tend to encourage it) as long as it is done with kindness. My classroom is not one in which I am the all knowing, all powerful, all encompassing person in charge. Yes, I run the classroom, but it is a place where all who come through the door are valued and allowed to question everything we do. That means I respect the people who walk into my classroom enough to tell them the truth, no matter what. If it is something that is more subjective, then we are all allowed to voice the differing viewpoints without recrimination. That doesn't mean we all get to trounce on each other's beliefs, instead it means we all will show the respect that is due by listening. In my way of thinking, even wrong answers deserve respect. Why do I operate that way? Because I truly believe that education is reciprocal. I learn as much from my students as they do from me. I would also rather hear the wrong answers or differing methods/opinions than hear nothing because the students are fearful of being told they are wrong. I still let them know when it is a wrong answer, but at least they are thinking about it.

How does this perfectly chaotic way of respecting everyone in the room manifest in classroom management? It is simply that my students end up with the freedom to think critically and express themselves because they know they are all valued. That is really the center of the respect issue for me. My students know I care about them because of who I am and what I do. They also feel free to ask the questions, give the opinions, question the methods, and speak up in the classroom because they know that they will be treated with respect regardless. In other words, I allow them the freedom to think critically because they won't be judged for doing it. Let's think about that for a second. We are all trying to get our students to think critically at some of the points in their lives when judgement around them is at an all time high. There are enough influences in the world showing people how to disagree and be ugly about it, in my classroom the respect we show supercedes that. It's ok to disagree. It's ok to get it wrong. Something my husband says all the time is that fail is not a word. It's an acronym and really means first attempt in learning. I know he didn't come up with that, but it is something we believe wholeheartedly in our classroom. I say our classroom because part of respecting each other as humans means we have collective ownership of things. Don't get me wrong, they have their things and I have my things, but we operate under the concept of ubuntu in the classroom. If you haven't heard the term, Ubuntu is an ancient African word meaning 'humanity to others'. It is often described as reminding us that 'I am what I am because of who we all are'. In other words, I am only a teacher because they are my students. That means they come into the classroom willing to learn and stretch their thinking. It is a collective endeavor that involves everyone. Sometimes you are the person that gets it first and easiest, sometimes you are the person that struggles. Either way, you are respected and valued and either help others or receive help. The chaos enters the equation because operating this way demands that flexibility exists and throwing away the thoughts of what respect looks like happens every day. You see, in our classroom, it's ok to stop in the middle of a lesson to explore it a little deeper. It's encouraged to ask why. It's a good thing to ask for help. It's even thought of as a positive to be passionate about a topic and show that passion. The chaos is in the noise and in the changing of the way that students think about school. It's in the interactions and the quest for knowledge that happen when some of the constraints are taken off the students. It's the freedom to fail and the support to keep trying.

17

Our classroom doesn't look like a cookie cutter classroom. You know what, that is ok. I'm not a cookie cutter teacher and they aren't cookie cutter students. Do we live within constraints of society, state legislation, school policies, etc.? Absolutely. Do we make that look at little different as we do it? You bet. Do they learn? 100% of them learn. They may not all be as successful in proving their knowledge, but they all learn. Guess what. I do, too. I learn from the students and the interactions. Do they fail? Yep. Do I? Yep. Do we all keep moving forward? Absolutely. Do we all grow as people? Every. Single. Day. We have to. If we are all in it together (last time I checked, we all had to inhabit this world together) then don't we owe it to each other to respect the humanity that is before us? Couldn't this world do with a little bit of learning to give respect even when we disagree?

You may be thinking, isn't this just teaching them to be good people? Yes, there is a part of this that is simply teaching them to be good people. Some of it might even be considered, dare I say it, Social Emotional Learning (SEL). Now, before you come at me, I realize SEL is getting a bad rap right now. Let's think about it though. Is SEL a new concept? Are the things taught in SEL brand new things? For the most part, no. SEL is just what teachers have been doing for as long as I have been alive. If we have been doing this forever, then why is there a sudden pushback? I think the answer to that question has more to do with mandating SEL than teaching it and I think it has to do with the fact that it has a name and an acronym and might allow different points of view to be shown to children. Don't get me wrong, I think there are some things that probably should not be taught in a school setting. In general, teaching students to be a good person is something I am pretty much in favor of doing. Teaching them to try new things is something I am pretty much in favor of doing. Teaching students that they don't always have to be the one that is right or the one with the last word is something that I am pretty much in favor of doing. Teaching them how to listen and learn from the world around them is something that I am pretty much in favor of doing. Teaching them how to do all of this and be kind is something I will always be in favor of doing. Giving them the freedom to teach me all of these things is something I will always be in favor of doing.

That's really at the heart of this for me. Teaching by modeling that there is something to learn from everyone we encounter; that everyone we encounter should be valued as a human; that while there are organizational structures that give people hierarchical value, that hierarchical value does not equate to the value of a person; that it's ok to disagree; that you don't have to have the last word; and that passion is something that is too often tamped down in the name of respect when it should be embraced.

CHAOS MANAGEMENT: BUILDING STRUCTURE WITHIN THE CHAOS

You need chaos in your soul to give birth to a dancing star - Frederick Nietsche

If you read the last chapter, you are probably thinking it looks like one of the scenes from *Night at the Museum.* One of the ones right after Larry Daley (played by Ben Stiller) takes over as night guard and the museum comes to life and runs wild. You know, where the monkey steals the keys, the head from Easter Island calls him Dum Dum, the neanderthals set things on fire, the dinosaur bones chase him, the miniatures from the Ancient Roman civilization and the Wild West go to war with each other, and the Huns hunt him down. If you have seen this movie, then you know that this happens because he won't take the advice given to him about how to control the chaos from the people that have been there. The same thing will happen if you try to run your classroom like I run mine without taking advice from others or thinking about who your students are and what they are like. Moving your classroom into perfect chaos requires some pre-planning, some flexibility, a willingness to fail and start over, and some prayer. In *Night at the Museum,* Larry goes back to the older night guards (yes they turn out to be villains, but that's for another chapter), gets advice from them, and then finds his helpers. To move into this perfect chaos setting for the classroom, you will need to do some of the same things. In other words, you've got to get advice from people that have done something like this before, talk to people that know about things like school culture and policy for your specific school, and find your helpers. Yes, this requires help. It requires an administrator that is willing to let you try this. It requires people in classrooms next to you that don't flinch every time they hear a sound. It requires students that want to try something different. These are your helpers. Students in your classroom that are willing to learn to be open. Students that are willing to be vocal. It doesn't have to be all of your students, but you have to find a few at first. Here's a hint, don't just pick ones that will get the right answers or plant wrong answers. That's part of building the culture. Managing this kind of chaos is not the same as putting the whole school outside on the football field and trying to teach them. It does require some understandings to be in place. One of the things I do is to try to establish norms with my students. This helps with a couple of things. It lets me know what contributes positively to the learning environment for my students, it gives them a sense of ownership for classroom culture, and it sets the tone that I want their input and value their thoughts. That's a pretty good return on something that can be done in 10 minutes or less. Having them help to set the norms and expectations also helps as we go through the class with some self-regulation. I promised stories for you, and here is another one. When I was first teaching high school, I went in with some plans for norms for the classroom that I thought were going to make things smoother. I had it mapped out in my head, I had done it in my classroom before the students got there to see if there were any problems, I was super excited and felt like I had created something that was going to save us a ton of time. I was excited to see how it was going to go. My great big idea was to give them the norm of our call and response. When I needed their attention back to me, I would call out "We Are" and they would all call out "Wolves" (our school mascot). Then I explained it to them and got the first shock from being at that particular school. This was a new school. It was a magnet school. It had kids from all over the county in it. They didn't have an identity as wolves yet. They still identified as their zoned high schools and the mascots that they had thought about being their whole school career. While we were working on unifying the school, they weren't comfortable with that yet. I had 2 options. I could insist that we use what I had made up or we could discuss it and come up with something else. I chose to discuss it and come up with something else that was student-directed. We had a short discussion about wanting to move to wolves when they were ready, and then decided to use "We are" and then they answered with the county. This helped them have their identity and also pushed them to check in with each other to determine when they were all ready to be wolves. They learned to respect the feelings of everyone in the room about this change. I like to think that was the first step in teaching them empathy, but I may be giving too much credit to a simple exchange.

Collaboratively setting the norms is just one step in this move towards perfect chaos, but it has become a pretty significant one. That is what sets the tone for the class. I also don't read the syllabus to my students. I hit highlights, then I ask them what questions they have. Although my initial reason for doing it this way was because I hated when people read something like that to me, that way of doing things has stuck around because students appreciate not being read to about that kind of thing. I had several students say it made them feel like I had faith that they were capable of reading and understanding things and that it let them know that I was also open to questions when they have them. They also appreciated not having a whole day of just having policies read to them. I even give them a quiz in our Learning Management System over the syllabus that they can take as many times as they want to take it to get a perfect score. That starts everyone out with the opportunity to have a "win" in the classroom and build some confidence.

Let's think about some of the things you do on the first day (or first few days) of school.

- Are there things that you are currently doing that could move to something done collaboratively? What are they?

- Are your students walking into an environment where they will get the feeling that this is going to be a welcoming place for discussion and questioning? What are the barriers they are facing? What barriers are you facing?
- Do students see a list of don'ts as soon as they hit the door? If so, how can you reframe that?
- Are you giving them any sense of control or ownership in the classroom? If so, how?
- Are you working yourself to death to have everything perfectly created before they get there?
- How could collaboratively creating norms help with chaos?

Now that you have thought about those things, let's talk a little more about the chaos. What does chaos look like in your room currently? Think back to when we thought about what type of teacher you want to be. Does your classroom embody that? Let's think through that for a minute.

- What type of chaos do you want in your room?
- What is your definition of perfect chaos?

Now that I have you thinking, here's another tip to controlling the chaos. Ask questions. It's that simple (if only). Ok. So asking questions won't control anything, but it will tell you what you need to know to control the chaos. A colleague once said to me that if someone is struggling with academics, we help them; so why do we punish students when they are struggling with discipline issues before we try to help? That's what I mean by asking questions. Don't ask why they did that, ask what they were trying to accomplish. It all goes into functions of behavior if you want the background, but think about it. If we know what a student is trying to accomplish, then we can help redirect them to appropriate behavior or actions. This also (again) goes into building that relational bond with your students where they feel heard and valued. Obviously, this is not taking the place of immediate actions when things are too much, but what difference could it make for your students to know that you aren't just looking to punish, but instead to help support their needs?

COMBINING THE "PERFECT" AND THE "CHAOS"

We live in two worlds - order and chaos. In the world of order, we plan, reflect, and think about what to do next. In the world of chaos, things happen, we get things done, yet unpredictability persists. In one world, we like to think we are in control. In the other, we mingle together with increasing complexity, conflict, and uncertainty. – David Spangler

At this point, you may be asking yourself how do I even do this? I think this is the teacher I want to be, but I don't know how to find my perfect chaos or how to break out of the mold that I have always heard teaching has to fit within to be effective. Go back to your reflections that you have done so far. What are your non-negotiables? If you are going to combine the perfect and the chaos, then you have to know where the line gets drawn in the sand. These next few pages are going to be prompts for you to work through. You can think of this as building your dream classroom or perfect world, but let yourself think outside the box. We will rein it back in later, but for now there really is no limit.

Structuring the Chaos (Creating Order in Exploration)

- What are my non-negotiables? *(What routines, expectations, or learning goals must remain consistent?)*

- How can I give students freedom while keeping them accountable? *(What tools or check-ins can help manage progress?)*

- What scaffolding do my students need before I let them explore? *(Do they need background knowledge or guidelines before diving in?)*

- How will I guide students back if they get too off-track? *(What signals will I use to redirect learning without stifling creativity?)*

Encouraging Creative Problem-Solving (Letting Students Take Risks)

- How can I create "safe chaos" where students feel comfortable experimenting? *(What strategies help normalize failure as part of learning?)*

- What structured choices can I provide to keep students engaged but focused? *(Should I use choice boards, tiered assignments, or project-based learning?)*

- How can I design assessments that reward both creativity and accuracy? *(Can students demonstrate mastery in multiple ways?)*

- What's the right balance between structure and flexibility in this classroom? *(Should I provide step-by-step guidance or just key checkpoints?)*

Technology & AI as a Bridge Between Order and Innovation (Let's save ourselves a little time)

- How can AI help me personalize structure while allowing exploration? *(Can AI tools provide personalized pacing while I facilitate inquiry-based learning?)*

- How can I use technology to manage "organized chaos"? *(Should I use collaborative digital boards, self-paced learning apps, or AI-assisted feedback?)*

- What AI tools can I introduce without overwhelming students? *(Which tools align with my goals instead of adding unnecessary complexity?)*

Classroom Culture & Mindset Shifts

- How do I prepare students to handle ambiguity and open-ended challenges? *(Do they need practice with problem-solving frameworks like design thinking?)*

- What classroom norms will help students thrive in a less rigid environment? *(How do I build a culture of respect, responsibility, and curiosity?)*

- How do I model adaptability and a growth mindset? *(How can I show that I am learning and experimenting with them?)*

- What cultural, geographical, or regional things do I need to keep in mind that are specific to my area and my students?

Norms & Expectations for Respectful Chaos

- How do I set clear expectations for open discussions and risk-taking?

  Example: Establish discussion norms like "Challenge ideas, not people."

- How do I ensure every student's voice is heSard, even in a chaotic setting?

  Example: Use structured turn-taking or digital collaboration tools to involve quieter students.

- How do I handle disagreements productively?
  Example: Teach conflict resolution strategies like "Listen, Restate, Respond."

Embracing Diverse Perspectives & Tolerating Differences

- How do I encourage students to engage with ideas they disagree with?

  Example: Use role-playing or structured debates where students argue both sides of an issue.

- How do I help students separate critique from personal attack?

  Example: Use sentence starters like "I see your point, but I wonder if..." to reframe disagreements.

- How can I highlight diverse experiences and voices in lessons?

  Example: Use AI-generated or real-world case studies from multiple cultural perspectives.

Managing Student Behavior & Emotional Safety

- How do I ensure that tolerance doesn't mean tolerating harmful behavior?

  Example: Have a clear distinction between free expression and disrespect, with consistent consequences.

- How do I support students who feel uncomfortable in an open-ended, less-structured environment? *Example: Provide opt-in structured alternatives or scaffolding for students who need more guidance.*

- How do I teach self-regulation and emotional awareness in an unpredictable learning space? *Example: Use mindfulness breaks or reflection journals to help students manage frustration.*

Perhaps the most important question that you need to reflect on is:

- How am I going to teach my students to do this? *(Finding and embracing your classroom's perfect chaos will not happen overnight and will push your students to think in ways that they may not have been accustomed to thinking previously. Think through what this looks like. Is it modeling, what kind of patience is going to be necessary?)*

ADDING IN A LITTLE LOGIC (AND MAYBE A LITTLE TECHNOLOGY, TOO)

I have great belief in the fact that whenever there is chaos, it creates wonderful thinking. I consider chaos a gift. – Septima Poinsette Clark

How to Keep Chaos From Becoming a Hot Mess

The thing about "Perfect Chaos" is that it looks different in every classroom. What works for one teacher might be a total disaster for another, and that's okay! Here's how to make it your own:

Different Grades, Different Vibes

o Elementary: Lots of movement, storytelling, hands-on projects.

o Middle School: Inquiry-based learning, hands-on activities, student-led projects.

o High School: More independent learning, open discussions, problem-solving tasks.

Adjusting for Your Subject

o Math? Think real-world problems and interactive tools.

o Science? Get students experimenting and asking big questions.

o Language Arts? Let them explore ideas through discussion and creativity.

Finding the Right Balance

o Keep key routines in place to anchor the chaos.

o Let students help set class norms so they feel ownership.

o Use structured freedom—choice boards, project-based learning, or flexible seating.

Real-Life Examples of "Perfect Chaos"

o A class where students work on different projects at different speeds.

o A flipped classroom where students learn at home and apply it in class.

o A classroom where students lead discussions and drive their learning.

Measure and Adjust

o Use quick check-ins and reflections to see if students are engaged.

o Track learning outcomes—are students actually grasping the material?

o If something isn't working, adapt rather than abandon the approach.

MAKING "PERFECT CHAOS" WORK IN YOUR CLASSROOM

Chaos is great—until it's not. You want energy and engagement, not total anarchy. Here's how to keep the balance:

Know Your Comfort Level

o   Some teachers thrive on spontaneity; others need more structure.

o   If you're not sure, start small and build up to more flexible approaches.

Set Boundaries Without Killing the Fun

o   Have anchor routines that give students a sense of security.

o   Offer structured choices instead of unlimited freedom.

Keep the Chaos Productive

o   Have clear checkpoints so students stay on track.

o   Use timers, visual cues, or tech tools to help keep things flowing.

o   Scaffold learning so students aren't lost in too many open-ended tasks.

Recognize When It's Too Much

o   If students are more frustrated than engaged, something's off.

o   If learning isn't happening, adjust your approach.

o   If you're constantly reacting instead of guiding, it's time to reset.

Use Data to Keep It in Check

o   Check student performance—if they aren't making progress, tweak your approach.

o   Gather student feedback—are they overwhelmed or thriving?

o   Track engagement levels—high energy is good, but are they actually learning?

Pulling It Back When Needed

o   Take a pause and reset classroom norms.

o   Talk with students about what's working and what's not.

o   Tweak things based on feedback—this is a process, not a one-time setup.

The goal isn't perfection—it's making learning engaging, fun, and effective while keeping yourself sane. Embrace the chaos, but don't be afraid to rein it in when needed!

BUILDING A CLASSROOM TECH PLAN WITHOUT LOSING YOUR MIND

So, you want to use technology in your classroom, but you don't want it to turn into a never-ending cycle of troubleshooting Wi-Fi, fighting with outdated devices, or getting overwhelmed by a million new tools? Totally understandable. A classroom tech plan is basically your way of making sure technology works for you, not the other way around.

This idea comes from my book *Educational Technology: Big Pictures and Practical Applications for the Classroom*, and it's a great way to set yourself up for success. Here's what you need to think about:

What's the Goal?

o   Why are you using technology? (Spoiler: "Because everyone else is" is not a good enough reason.)

o   Are you trying to make learning more interactive? Give students more independence? Make grading easier?

What Do You Already Have?

o   What tech is available? Think about devices, software, Wi-Fi, and access at home.

o   What are the gaps? Not enough Chromebooks? Poor internet? Limited teacher training?

Choosing the Right Tools

o Pick tech that actually supports your teaching style and goals.

o Don't get distracted by the latest flashy app—ask yourself, "Will this make learning better?"

Making It Happen

o Plan out how you'll introduce new tools without overwhelming yourself or your students.

o Consider training for both teachers and students—if no one knows how to use the tech, it won't help.

Keeping It Safe and Smooth

o Set clear rules for how and when students use tech.

o Think about digital safety, privacy, and making sure all students have access.

Adjust as Needed

o Use student feedback and data to see what's working and what's not.

o If something isn't improving learning, ditch it and try something else—no guilt required.

FIGURING OUT WHAT YOU'VE GOT AND HOW TO USE IT

Before you go dreaming up a high-tech utopia for your classroom, take a step back and figure out what's actually possible with the resources you have. Here's how:

Take Inventory

o What devices do you and your students have access to? (School-owned? BYOD?)

o What apps and platforms does your school already use?

o Do students have reliable internet at home?

What's Missing?

o Do you have enough devices for all students?

o Is everything up-to-date and functional, or are you dealing with ancient tech?

o Do students need assistive technology?

Stretch What You've Got

o Use free tools whenever possible (Google Suite, Kahoot, Flip, etc.).

o Apply for grants or reach out to local businesses for donations.

o Get creative—pair students on devices, rotate tech use, or create offline options.

Get Everyone On Board

o   Make sure you and your students know how to use the tech you have.

o   Appoint student tech experts to help classmates troubleshoot.

o   Set up simple routines so tech doesn't become a classroom distraction.

Check the Data

o   Track student progress using tech-based assessments.

o   Use feedback surveys to find out what's actually helping students learn.

o   Be willing to tweak or replace tools that aren't working.

NO MORE COOKIE-CUTTER TEACHING

Teaching is not about molding students into a single shape—it's about guiding them to discover their own paths. No more cookie-cutter education; real learning happens when we follow their lead. – Ronda Blevins

You see, I've been that teacher that was trying my best to be just like someone else. I'm not writing this book because there need to be a ton of Ronda clones out there teaching. The world needs the teachers that have it all together. I am only able to be who I am because I felt like I had permission to be me. I'm a people pleaser and a perfectionist. Yeah, it's a horrible combo, I know. I felt like I needed permission to be who I am when I teach. I was lucky enough to be surrounded by people that gave me that permission. They didn't do it because they needed to give me permission, they did it because they knew I needed it. If that is you, here it is.

Teaching is not about molding students into a single shape—it's about guiding them to discover their own paths. No more cookie-cutter education; real learning happens when we follow their lead.

I've been that teacher who tried to fit into someone else's mold. I've stared at the perfectly organized classrooms, the teachers with their Pinterest-worthy bulletin boards and flawlessly structured lesson plans, and thought, "Maybe if I do it their way, I'll finally get it right." But the truth is, teaching isn't about finding the 'right' way—it's about finding your way. And that way will look different for every single teacher.

You don't need permission to be yourself in your classroom, but if you're anything like me, maybe you've been waiting for it. So here it is: You have permission to teach in a way that feels authentic to you. You have permission to create your own version of the ideal learning environment. You have permission to embrace the chaos, the creativity, the spontaneity, and the joy that make learning meaningful.

There's a myth that great teaching has to look a certain way—structured, quiet, predictable. But what if real learning thrives in the unpredictable? What if students engage best when they are encouraged to move, explore, and question? What if 'perfect' isn't a neat, orderly classroom, but one filled with energy, curiosity, and growth? That's what I call Perfect Chaos— the balance between structure and freedom that allows both teachers and students to thrive.

Perfect Chaos doesn't mean anarchy. It doesn't mean abandoning all structure and letting students run wild. It means understanding that learning isn't linear. It's messy, noisy, and sometimes unpredictable. It means recognizing that what works for one class, one student, or even one day might not work the next. And that's okay. Teaching isn't about perfection—it's about progress.

So how do you break free from the cookie-cutter mold?

Accept That You're Not Every Other Teacher

You don't have to teach like the person down the hall. You don't have to fit into a one-size-fits-all system. You became a teacher because you had a vision for how learning should be. Trust that vision. Trust yourself.

Build a Classroom That Reflects You

Your classroom doesn't have to look like a page from a catalog to be effective. Maybe your students sit in flexible seating arrangements. Maybe you start each class with a conversation instead of a worksheet. Maybe you teach math outside using sidewalk chalk. If it works for your students, it's the right way.

Give Students Ownership

Perfect Chaos means students have a say in how they learn. Let them help set classroom norms. Let them choose how they demonstrate their knowledge. Let them explore their own interests within the curriculum. When students feel ownership over their learning, they engage more deeply.

Use Data, But Don't Be Defined by It

Data is important. It tells us what's working and what's not. But data should guide your teaching, not dictate it. If students are struggling, pivot. If they're thriving, push them further. Your instincts as a teacher are just as valuable as any standardized assessment.

Find Joy in the Chaos

Learning should be joyful. If you're exhausted from trying to force everything into a neat little box, maybe it's time to rethink the box itself. Let go of the need to control every aspect of your classroom. Trust the process. Trust your students. And most importantly, trust yourself.

No more cookie-cutter teaching. No more trying to fit into someone else's expectations. Find your version of Perfect Chaos and own it. Your students don't need a perfect teacher—they need a real one. And that's exactly who you're meant to be.

PERMISSION GIVEN

Here is your permission to be the teacher you wrote about and dream of being. It is your permission to not have it all together all the time. It is your permission to put your desks in circles or get rid of them all together and use a different form of seating. You have permission to create your perfect chaos. If you want to use a free game on your phone to teach something to your students, go for it (as long as it points to your standards/objectives). If you dream of being the teacher that uses relational teaching, listens to students, and combines education and engagement in a way that students typically describe as fun but can be backed as true learning with data, then let this be the empowerment that you need to tackle that. You don't have to be the cookie-cutter teacher. There are teachers out there like you. Maybe you are becoming/became a teacher through an alternative path, maybe you teach a different discipline than everyone else, maybe you just want to teach math by going outside with sidewalk chalk to collect things and draw graph and all of those things are great and you should go for it. Don't let a standardized definition of teaching define you. We differentiate for students. Yes, you should be utilizing data to make certain your students are learning. Guess what... Every teacher should be doing that, regardless of being Type A, B, C, or Z. Use the data and your knowledge of your students and make certain they are learning. Don't let the chaos overwhelm, even if it is perfect. Embrace who you are and the teacher you have always wanted to be and find your Perfect Chaos.

ABOUT THE AUTHOR

Dr. Ronda M. Blevins is an educator and mentor dedicated to preparing future teachers and supporting current educators in their professional growth. She focuses on building strong relationships, promoting innovative and practical teaching strategies, and fostering real-world learning experiences. Her passion lies in helping teachers develop confidence, resilience, and a student-centered mindset that drives lasting impact in the classroom. Through collaboration, reflection, and ongoing support, she works to ensure educators are equipped to meet the diverse needs of today's learners while continuing to grow in their practice throughout their careers.

www.ingramcontent.com/pod-product-compliance
Lightning Source LLC
Chambersburg PA
CBHW051245120626
46547CB00014B/1805